If I could go back

20 things I wish I knew as a new parent

Contents

For my first pancake child, Barclay. You turned out more than alright.

Introduction

38 hours after having my first baby, after a hospital stay where loud nurses checked on me every 15 minutes and had me track every pee, poop, and feeding, a tired woman pushed me to the curb in a wheelchair...and let me go home with a real live baby.

I couldn't believe it. I couldn't believe I didn't have to take a class or get a certification in order to qualify for parenthood. I knew people who adopted dogs who had to do more training to prove that they were capable. As the oldest of 7 children, I knew how to change a diaper in my sleep, but guiding a human to adulthood? Terrifying.

As soon as my belly was round enough for people to know I was going to be a mother, the advice was pouring in. I was given books to read, methods to follow, and to be honest, constantly warned about how awful it was going to be.

You'll never sleep again.

You'll never get your body back.

You won't be able to travel or finish your coffee or pee alone.

I'll never forget, a few years later, standing in the

checkout line at Target with a screaming toddler clutching my thigh and a newborn baby rooting at my milk-soaked shirt and a lady staring at me with fire in her eyes.

"It gets worse. Just wait till they are teenagers," she warned.

On the flip side, if someone wasn't griping about the bad parts of parenting, they were telling me to savor every moment during those times I surely didn't want to savor. It got to the point that if a gray-haired lady approached me in public, I would start to brace myself.

There are millions of ways to raise children. And there are millions of different children to raise.

Despite all these differences, the thing that unites us all as parents is this sentiment: if we could go back and try again, we would do some things differently.

A bit about me

This book is not based on scientific research. It is not composed of multiple experiences gathered from research groups at a university. This book gives no step-by-step guides, it makes no promises.

This is a book about me: a mother to 3, a birth and postpartum doula, and someone who lives with the attitude of *it takes a village*.

This book is made up of both things I did well and ways I wish I did better. I have come to a place of great self-compassion as I think back on ways I've regretted interacting with my children. I've been told many times, "Parenting is doing the best you can, with the knowledge you have." That kind of sucks. I wish so much that I knew more. I wish that I had not been doing so much of my own healing while being responsible for little lives. Basically, it wasn't until kid #3 that I started to feel like I was getting the hang of it, and there are days I wish I could go back to my poor first child to do better.

But that's not how it works.

I've sat with many new parents on the cusp of their

births, and in my stumbly, awkward way I have shared what has worked for me when they ask about parenting. I have seen that mother in the Target check-out line and stepped in to help her to her car, or I've told a dad at the playground he was doing a great job, and, if I get half a margarita in me, I can often be found telling the couple next to me with a 2-year-old,

"It gets better!"

I've written this book for you, the parents. We don't have to buy into this lie that parenting is a chore, that we need to grit our teeth to make it through. We don't have to spend our days in a ball of anxiety because we don't know what the right thing to do is. We will make mistakes, that is a given, but we can raise children and enjoy doing it. That is my desire for you: to give you some much needed hope and perspective, to give you permission to enjoy your children in the midst of the inevitable chaos and mess.

Raising babies is wild. Not just because of how rapidly children grow and change, but because of how absolutely transformative it is to you, the parent.

I realize not everyone comes to parenthood through pregnancy, but I am including chapters on pregnancy and birth simply because I have had the honor of being in those spaces for many years and have witnessed hundreds of families grow in that manner.

I also want to acknowledge that I often write from the perspective of a mother, because I am one. But this book is for any parent, for anyone tasked with the role of raising children. Gender, biological DNA sharing, and circumstance do not matter.

This book also has some religious undertones, as I was raised in a strict evangelical home. I now have my own faith that I have untangled from what I was taught, but I have purposely not included any sort of faith-based parenting in this book because I know that it often brings complexity, grief, and might even make you put this book back on the shelf.

Lastly, I talk a lot about my oldest son in these pages. Much more than my other two children. This is simply because I did most of my learning on him. I wrote this book with his permission to share.

All said and done, take it or leave it, here's what I would do if I could go back and do it again.

You don't need stuff to have a baby, you need support and a positive frame of mind

When I think of my first pregnancy I do not think about that one day that I managed to not puke on myself. The day I wore a long flowing red dress and posed for photos in some abandoned field that I definitely trespassed on with the sun illuminating me like some sort of goddess. No, I think about feeling really alone. Of being in the produce section of the grocery store and hurling into a produce bag because I glimpsed a head of lettuce. Of wondering how there were so many humans on earth that all came into existence this way and yet I felt like I was the first person to ever feel the wide range of feelings growing a human brought. I think about buying overpriced onesies at Old Navy every time I felt scared or ill prepared. I was craving deep connection and encouragement and instead my growing belly was the start of horror stories, warnings, and opinions on everything from complete strangers. I don't know why, but in a brief elevator interaction, a pregnant person will hear tales of ripping perineums, opinions on drugs, and comments about their size before they've even reached their floor.

The second I found out I was pregnant everything

changed for me. I remember my heart beating so fast for days as suddenly my future was rearranged to include a baby. I was absolutely bursting with giddiness about becoming a mother; it felt like nothing could bring me down from cloud 9. However, this unbridled joy became hard to keep as my belly grew.

You'll never sleep.
You'll never get your body back.
Say goodbye to everything you hold dear.
You've gained too much weight.
You're probably too short to have a vaginal delivery.
My friend's, neighbor's, mother's baby died at birth.
Don't even think about trying to go without an epidural.
I hate your baby's name.

The funny thing is that all those people who took every chance to bemoan having a baby also wanted to put that aside for a day to have a party. That one day they would all flock to sip on too-sweet punch and play god awful baby shower games involving giant safety pins or even worse, candy bars melted in diapers. It has become such a rite of passage to sit uncomfortably in front of all the women in your life and slowly and awkwardly open 37 onesies and 27 blankets slowly to a chorus of high pitched oooohs and ahhhs. Then about the time everyone has guessed the weight of your baby, which I truly don't understand the obsession with, you're opening nipple pads and butt cream.

In this modern age, so much of our energy, money, and time is spent on physical things: the newest must-have gadget, the latest swaddle wrap that promises your baby will sleep through the night, the first sippy cup in the history of the world that doesn't leak. Capitalism loves new parents. It's a billion-dollar industry that takes advantage of the vulnerable state that comes with a new baby. Because of the way we live, walled up in our own homes, showing only the highlight reel in our social media feeds, parenthood is a great mystery to most people. Having and buying stuff makes us *feel* prepared when in fact it distracts us from gathering wisdom and encouragement from those who have done it before. And those who have gone before us feel like they've done enough when they click that Amazon wish-list link. Meanwhile there is a chasm of disconnect surround the whole process.

An alternative to the traditional baby shower is a Blessingway. I personally didn't experience this myself as a pregnant mother, but where I live many people have one. This is a very sacred ritual in which people gather and bless the family before the baby arrives, a radical departure from the consumer-obsessed baby showers most people have. The clients that I have had who have experienced this beautiful ceremony have come to their birth with a feeling of community, with a feeling of not being alone, with a feeling of being held. Oftentimes women all over the community will light a candle to burn during the labor time, blowing it out when the baby is finally born. I've also had friends wear a red string around their wrists that they do not cut until the baby comes, symbolizing connection. Folks who attend often give a donation for a birth doula, or set up nourishing meals to allow the family to enjoy their baby in the postpartum. Because I promise you, you don't need fifty 0–3-month onesies. But you would so greatly benefit from the support of a birth and postpartum doula. You surely do not need the latest wipe warmer, but instead could use a friend or a sister to distract you while you wait for labor to start. So many baby items will remain unused, which you thought you needed, but you will never have enough people showing up, whether physically or emotionally, during the hazy first weeks of figuring it out.

The best way you can prepare for parenthood is

surrounding yourself with the right people. It might be family; it might be chosen family made up of friends. It might include putting up boundaries with people who drain your energy, judge you, or bring negativity.

Near the end of pregnancy, when I sit with people to discuss their upcoming birth, I talk to them about what I call "the stretching time". If you are carrying a baby, this also includes physical stretching. This is the weeks leading up to when your baby is born, that limbo stage, that waiting time. A lot of people talk about the hard parts: not sleeping because you have to pee so much, swelling, or the feeling of being out of control. While some of those things will happen, balancing this waiting period with deep, unapologetic rest and fun things to look forward to can make this time sacred and precious. Days can easily bleed together in a restless and impatient way if you're simply pausing your life to wait, but being intentional about staying connected with loved ones, deepening your connection with your partner, and holding on to life's simple pleasures will ensure that you start your parenting journey in a good frame of mind.

I always tell parents that it's better to cancel something because you're going into labor (and I promise you that is a great excuse to get out of anything) than it is to not plan anything at all. These sprinkles of connection, these glimmers of enjoyment can be free: a walk with a friend, inviting people over to dinner, exploring a nearby town. Or you can splurge a little with a massage, a special tea, or shopping with a friend for some cozy new pjs. This waiting time is also a good time for sleeping extra if possible, binging a show, or just enjoying slowing down and allowing yourself to lean into this holy season of life-bringing.

I am not saying it will be easy. In fact, I can promise you it might feel like an uphill battle some days. Today if you say the words "pregnant" or "baby" around your devices you will be bombarded with advice, ads, and niche marketing that will wear your down. But try to not get sucked into thinking that you need *things* to prepare for your baby. Instead, focus on surrounding yourself with people who encourage and support you and help you to get yourself into a positive frame of mind.

Get yourself a good team and surrender

Birth is a death. There is just no way around it. You will not find this written in a nursery cross stitch or on birth mantra cards, but as a doula who has witnessed hundreds of births and also as someone who has birthed my own three babies, it is the truest thing I know. Birth is a death the way trees lose their leaves in the winter...in order that bright new leaves can grow.

I was the first of any of my friends to have a baby. I had a dear friend who would often say, "Please don't change. Please don't become one of *those* moms." I tried my best to keep up my identity even though my body was changing. I struggled to keep food down for the entire pregnancy, and I thought about my baby and our future nearly every moment of the day. After a 50-hour labor, that friend joyfully snuck margaritas into the hospital to celebrate. I remember holding the glass in one hand and my baby awkwardly in the other hand and toasting to the this new life, even though I felt like I had died in a way. I hadn't slept in 50 hours, my lidocaine from 12 stitches was wearing off, and I found myself so transformed by the experience that I simply wasn't the same person, I had been reborn alongside this baby. I didn't want my friend to know. About 2 weeks later she took me for tacos and more margaritas in a town an hour away. I was shaking with exhaustion, and the responsibility of keeping a whole human alive was constantly blowing my mind. I could barely walk, my nipples were cracked, and I tried nursing under a cover as I chatted away and sipped my drink. I tried to pretend I had it all figured out and could continue on as if nothing had happened. Halfway through lunch I felt a pool of warm liquid on my thigh and looked down to see that my baby had been latched to the side of my nipple, had given me a giant hickey, and all my milk had poured onto my skirt. Later I sat in the changing room of a Macy's as my friend tried on dresses and thought to myself, "I don't know that I can keep this up."

It was several weeks before I succumbed to the power of birth and who it had chiseled me into. Suddenly I moved from frustrated to empowered. With each subsequent birth I experienced, I learned to let it do its work and to not fight the way it would change me.

Pregnancy and birth are teachers and the lesson is that no matter what, we are not in control. After supporting families in this journey for more than a decade, I've learned it is sometimes painful to watch as everyone (even the most prepared people) have to open their hands to surrender. Sometimes it's beautiful, sometimes it's full of grief, but babies don't come without it.

I've sat in many homes before the birth, and listened to the fears and the hesitant excitement of the unknown. Often their home is picked up, a fresh plate of fruit offered to me, a perfectly made crib is usually set up in a nursery flooded with unboxed baby gear. We talk about their wishes, the way they want to bring their little one into the world, we make a birth intentions list and I leave, telling them this:

It's ok to imagine the best birth you can, because I will hold all the possibilities of pivots until we need to talk about them.

This might not go to plan.

I will support you no matter what.

I can help a woman having her sixth baby, who experienced the same type of birth for all 5 previous children and then that stubborn sixth baby could throw a curve ball and come in their very own unique way. A woman who runs marathons like its breathing can struggle for days. People who "do everything right" can have unexpected hurdles show up and need an emergency cesarian birth. And for a lot of people, it can unfold without any intervention at all.

Setting up a supportive and knowledgeable birth team is key in allowing you to surrender safely. You need to be able to trust them. I am and will always be a huge advocate of birth doulas. A birth doula is someone that supports the parents emotionally and physically during the birth. The physical support is not medical, but more nurturing (like massage, hip squeezes, giving sips of water, holding them). Doulas statistically reduce your probability of a cesarean birth, reduce the need of interventions, and most importantly, people who have doulas are much more likely to have a positive birth experience no matter how their baby comes into the world.

In the end, the difference between a beautiful birth story and a traumatic one, is not *how* you birth your baby—but how you *feel* when you birth your baby.

I've seen women who had the quintessential, idealistic, calm (looking) water birth describe their experience as flying alone through the darkness of space, and simply recalling it to memory can cause intense emotions. And I've seen mothers laid out on operating tables who said this was the birth of their dreams. I, personally, felt the most joy and presence in an unexpected cesarean birth with my third baby, because I had a loving birth team that surrounded me from start to finish.

So get yourself a birth team—one that will hold your hands, give you the opportunity to open yourself up to the transformation that will occur, encourage you to let go of set in stone plans—while allowing you to feel safe and cared for.

For the birth of my first child, I thought I had prepared all I could. I had a good team, a local midwife practice with black and white photos of beautiful bellies adorning the walls and a feeling of generational wisdom in its foundation. What I didn't plan on was giving birth during an ice storm with 5 other women. Even though my midwife was lovely, she was stretched so thin that night and I found myself going through the process blind and with a nurse who was annoyed with my whimpers. Every few hours my midwife would come to be with me and immediately get called to someone else who needed her more. What I needed was constant support; we all need constant support.

A lot of people think that doulas only attend hippy-dippy home births and are anti-drugs. This couldn't be further from the truth. When I show up to a birth, I have no agendas of my own. I've been hired for cesarian births, planned epidural births with as many drugs as possible, and intimate home births. And I love them all.

I will never forget showing up to a birth where the plan was to have a second unmedicated birth. I showed up ready to go and the mom, who was very connected to her intuition, informed me, "I am changing my mind today. I don't feel like having an unmedicated birth today." She ended up getting an early epidural and we spent the entire birth laughing and telling stories. There were even times I stepped back because she and her husband were experiencing such unexpected emotional intimacy in the absence of pain. She knew that was exactly what she needed that day and had she stuck to her birth plan, it wouldn't have unfolded in the beautiful way it did.

I had another client once who was planning to birth her second baby in a tub at a birth center and ended up at a nearby hospital having a cesarean birth (turns out she had a grapefruit cyst that was not allowing her baby to come out). Her husband and I held her for hours as she labored, we did everything right. She did everything right. The drastic 180 from the plan was shocking. I held her as they were taking her back and kissed her like she was my sister. This mama spent months wrestling with the complex feelings of knowing the traumatic experience of her birth was life saving for her baby. She grieved. As weeks and months came and went, she found herself releasing the grip of control. That birth ended up being the catalyst to her coming into a season of deep authenticity and freedom that couldn't have come had she held tight to who she was, had she not let the death happen.

She told me, "Surrendering to the way he had to come took away all the makeshift walls that I was protecting myself with." This revelation came one day, after finding unexpected gratitude in the aftermath of things not going to plan.

Partners also do not escape this transformation, because this is their birth too. I have seen incredible change come over the shyest of partners as they too surrender their lack of control and let their birth experience empower them. I have seen the most unsure of fathers grow in front of my eyes as I guide their hand to the perfect spot to press on their partner's back. I have seen partners frozen in fear as they watch their love do the hard work they can't do themselves.

When I go for my postpartum visit, there are often tears, milk or poop stained clothes, and dishes piled in the sink. I will use this time to talk about their birth story. I keep track of special moments to remind them of things said and done.

As we recall these moments, we will cry or laugh with the memory. We allow space for parts that were scary and parts that empowered them. If they were well supported, many partners have a deepening of love for each other from the experience. In the hundreds of births I have attended, no matter how the birth unfolded, I have never found someone unchanged from it.

3

Parenthood can be two things at once

The high of my first med free birth decided to wear off at TJ Maxx. I had an energetic 2-year-old babbling in my cart and a chunky 10 day old strapped to my chest. My husband was taking a class in a nearby town and I had come along to swim in the hotel pool and eat take out. I had browsed for what felt like days as every single ounce of energy drained from my postpartum body. I remember walking the aisle and nodding as people admired my offspring. By the time I made it to the check out with a tiny red toy airplane and some popcorn, I could barely hold myself up.

"Hi there, welcome to TJ Maxx, will you be using your TJ Maxx credit card to save 10% today?"

"Ummm can you call the police to come take care of my children so I can take a nap in my car?"

The words spilled out of my mouth without any regard to etiquette.

That middle-aged woman with a choppy short haircut and a thin mustache stared into my soul. Her mouth sort of fell open in slow motion. We stood there in suspended purgatory before I snapped out of it and forced out a laugh so that she didn't take me seriously.

I did manage to make it to my car to buckle the kids in before I slumped over my steering wheel for who knows how long of a power nap.

Just a day before I had easily done a 3 mile hike and was bragging to my sister about how good I felt. Even as a more seasoned second time mom, I had tried to fit my experiences into very neat little boxes of "good" and "bad".

A lot of what you will hear in your parenting journey comes from two different camps:

Just you wait…

and

Enjoy every minute. . .it goes too fast.

I would be pregnant and someone would say, "Oh just you wait, you feel tired now? It gets so much worse!"

I would have a newborn and would be bleary eyed with exhaustion and someone would say, "Oh you think this is hard? Wait till they start moving."

When I had a crawler, the "just you waits" would flood in for the walking stage.

Just wait till they are in the terrible twos

Just wait till they are a THREENAGER

Just wait till they can talk back.

Just wait till school starts

Just wait until they are teenagers.

While this impending doom loomed ahead of me AT ALL TIMES, I was also being told by the other half of the population to enjoy every minute because one day I would be old, sad, and wishing I was back to the exact stage I was at now.

This leaves us parents in a state of paralysis as we straddle the fear of what's to come with the fear of not enjoying what is.

Let me tell you, I am a decade removed from any sort of newborn days and while I do have the fond memories of newborn smell, soft coos, and no talking back, the bone-tired feelings of exhaustion is not something I miss at all.

What if we entered each new stage of childhood with a blank slate, knowing how that stage holds both beautiful aspects and challenging aspects? What if we allowed for a dualistic experience in this wild journey? What if we wait to see what unfolds? What if we rode the waves that inevitably come instead of trying to get out of the water?

You can be grateful to grow life in your womb AND feel sad that your body changed.

You are allowed to both feel love drunk AND be frustrated that you have to wake up in the night to feed a new baby.

We can enjoy the precious lisps of a toddler figuring out how to talk AND wish that you could spend an entire day in a silent monastery.

You can love the messes that creative kindergartners make AND look forward to the day when they can clean up after themselves.

We can miss when our kids were little and needed us more AND enjoy the freedom of having a teenager.

What if instead of spending our long days panicked that we aren't enjoying it all enough, we allowed ourselves to feel both? What if we allowed our emotions to enter and leave each stage without judgment or guilt?

I can tell you what happens. It allows you to move through hard times. It opens you up for support when you need it. Finally, it gives space for you to enjoy and cherish moments that you might have missed had you been trying to pretend that everything was perfect when it wasn't. That's the thing. This hologram of everything being perfect robs us of enjoying what is. Letting two things be true ultimately gives way to allowing you to be present. And being present allows you to move through life with fewer regrets.

4

The greatest gift you can give your children is taking care of yourself

I grew up in evangelical Christianity. In this sect of religion, the biggest goal of a woman's life was to be a mother. And mothers stayed home, cooked and cleaned, and gave everything to their children. I remember sitting in the itchy green seats of church and watching families file into their rows, sometimes filling an entire row with one family. I was observant and I paid close attention to these women, these ragged and weary mothers. I listened to what they talked about, what they groaned about, what they hoped for. Rarely did I ever hear a woman think outside of her family. No one was working, no one was learning anything new. Their lives were divided into before motherhood and after. And the after involved a loss of self in a very significant way. While I realize not everyone had such a starkly conservative upbringing, I do think that very often parents tend to lose themselves when they have children.

I grew up with a very sacrificial mother. Her sacrifices started with my 60-hour birth at 2 weeks overdue and just never ended. She went without to feed me during times of scarcity, never pursued a career, and weeded my violin teacher's garden on a steep hill so I could have lessons. I am so grateful for her sacrifices and the love she poured out, but also, I didn't ask her to do it. In fact, if I had a choice, if 5-year-old me could communicate complex ideas, I would have told my mother I didn't care about the beautiful dinner she made from scratch if it meant she didn't get to take a walk on the beach. I would have chosen for her to nurture who she was as a person instead of emptying herself out and giving everything to me and my siblings.

I loved seeing my mom alive. I loved seeing her laugh or her cheeks flush with vitality. It was a rare site and I treasure all of those moments of glimpsing into who she was other than my mother.

I remember vividly when I was probably 10 years old, her telling me, "I had the opportunity to go out to lunch with some friends but I chose to stay home with you." I think she wanted me to be impressed with how much she had given up. I know she meant it out of love, but I remember feeling really sad and confused. I wanted her to go and I hated the fact that it was because of me that she didn't.

It's tragic really, this deep ache that she gave me everything at the expense of herself, and worst of all, that I didn't even want her to. In fact, I would venture to say that if children feel safety and attachment past their newborn days, that no child wants the burden of being your everything, your purpose for life. You can pour your love on them, but you are still you and they are still them.

When I became a parent, it was one of the biggest goals I had, to keep tending to myself as a person, finding my way to fit in doing hobbies I loved, connecting with people, and having new experiences. I was determined that my children would not feel like they were clipping my wings and in turn they wouldn't feel like my happiness was entirely wrapped up in them, that they wouldn't feel as if they were failing.

I do not regret keeping my own autonomy separate from my children. I did it awkwardly and imperfectly and who knows, in a decade when they might have their own children-they might want to swing the pendulum back a bit more. Being their mother is a privilege and certainly a calling, but it wasn't *who I was*. Clinging to this throughout many seasons of parenting has allowed for a lot of growth for all of us, and when they leave my home to live their own lives, I will be ok and they will be ok too.

As a doula I have seen parents 2 years in, agonizing over going on their first date night since the baby arrived, as if their baby could or would hold it against them. And yet when they return from date night they are both invigorated, having remembered that they are still themselves and I know that they will be better parents because of it. The ripples of this self-care are far reaching. It is fear, not love, that is keeping us stuck, telling us that wearing ourselves thin or ignoring our own human needs is what our children need.

No. Our children need whole, healthy, thriving parents who show them the importance of asking for help, taking breaks, resting, working through grief, and even making space to have fun. Our children need examples of healthy self-care.

The reality is that you will have to get creative to find time and space for this nurturing, especially when you have very little kids. Maybe you keep dinner simple, stay up an extra hour to chat with a friend, do a date night childcare swap with another family, skip Netflix to pick up your old watercolors, or do a virtual therapy session during nap time. If you are coparenting with someone, maybe pick nights of the week or month that you can take a class, go to a book club, even just sit outside on the porch and freaking breathe.

Good parenting does involve a great deal of giving up. Some days it might feel like the sacrifices never end.

However, making sure that you don't give up who you are as your own person will in turn be a gift to your children. It will reduce bitterness and ensure that when your nest is empty, you will not be left with remnants to piece together of who you used to be.

Ideas of ways to invest in yourself

- Sign up for a class about something you've always wanted to try (pottery, aerial silks, a creative writing workshop, a hip-hop class). Maybe it's only once a month, or maybe you have the resources to make a weekly class happen.
- Sprinkle guilty pleasures throughout your day. Have a ton of laundry you need to do during nap time? Give yourself 10 minutes of time on your porch just soaking up the sun. Have to finish work after the kids go to bed? Fix a big bowl of your favorite popcorn to eat while you do it. Play a favorite playlist when you're doing something boring.
- Keep learning. Watch a documentary about something you didn't know about. Research museums nearby, read a memoir from a time period you like, pop your ear buds in while you're washing dishes to listen to a podcast.
- Make and keep a date night. Maybe it's only once a month, maybe you can swing every week.

Reminder that dates do not have to equal money. Take a walk, see a free concert in the park, take a walk. If babysitting isn't in the budget, do a childcare trade with someone you trust.

- Host a potluck dinner with friends.
- Create a simple ritual to go alongside something you don't look forward to (ie make a nice cup of tea to drink when you're helping with homework).
- Go put your feet in the grass.
- Move your body (online yoga class, in person dance class, dancing to your favorite song from high school).
- Wear something that makes you feel most like yourself.
- Do something creative even if the end result is terrible.
- Call a friend you miss.
- Make therapy a priority. I believe that every parent could benefit from seasons of therapy. Feel uncomfortable with talk therapy? Try art therapy, group therapy, music therapy.
- Join a book club
- Get take out for dinner and watch a movie you've been wanting to see during your usual meal prep time.

5

Learning to trust yourself will make you a better parent

My grandmother gave birth to her 5 children while she was "asleep". As a high society woman in the 1950s she had the "privilege" of not having to feel the pain of childbirth by being put under heavy anesthesia and simply waking to a baby in the nursery. This trauma, and the lies of being told that only slaves and animals breastfed their babies, haunted her until her dying day. Parenting was hands off when my father and mother were being raised with very little coddling, holding, or bonding occurring. I still feel the sting and the ripple effects the lack of attachment they experienced contributed to. Growing up religious I was warned about spoiling babies or letting children think they were in charge. This authoritarian way of viewing child-rearing stole a lot of joy from me in the early months of my own mothering. It caused a lot of harm to me and to many people I grew up with.

Since having my first baby in 2009, attachment parenting has made a grand comeback and I'm grateful for it. In my own experience of raising 3 children, attachment is just another name for intuition. Creating space for nurturing this intuition makes parenting so much less of a guessing game. I hear people joke, "I didn't get a manual for this kid." But while that's true, we don't have a paper instruction manual to leaf through, we can sense what our children need infinitely more than any podcaster, author, or parenting expert. Working on attachment allows you to parent with the confidence that no one knows your child like you do.

The good and the bad news is that trust starts within your own self.

I think our intuition starts before the baby is even born, coming into our knowing, learning to sift through well-meaning advice, picking and choosing what works for your family and for your child, and letting the rest go. The problem is, humans have mostly lost touch with tuning into ourselves, so we often have little to no practice. Becoming a parent usually breaks us open and forces us to grow in a way that nothing else can. In my experience in supporting hundreds of families through this start to parenthood, I have been shocked at how many people have made it to adulthood with absolutely no intuitive skills. Learning to trust in your instincts and being ok with sometimes making mistakes, does take practice no matter how uncomfortable it is.

The truth of it is, there is absolutely no one-size-fits all method, no step-by-step guide that will fit every child, because every single child is unique.

The experience of having my first child was wildly different from my second. I remember many times holding him while he cried and thinking, "Where is this kid's mother?" I felt like a babysitter sometimes and I second-guessed everything I did. By the time my second son Sullivan came along I had done a lot of work putting aside productivity, people pleasing, and expectations. This saved a lot of frustration of me trying to push him through the same mold that my first born forged and instead felt like I could feel what he needed most of the time.

I held him often, fed him often, and settled into the blissful new chapter that I knew would not last forever. Of course it was chaotic at times with a 2-year-old running around, and of course there were times I felt inadequate or incapable, but in comparison to the first time, it was light years better.

I saw an interview the other day with a mom on Tik-Tok. She said that she would always let her children come to her bed if they were scared or worried about something. She would spend that time connecting to them, listening to them, and loving on them.

"I got a lot of hate for it." she said.

People would say, "Oh my goodness! What if they are still coming when they are in high school?"

She replied, "I would love my high schooler to feel comfortable to come to me like that!"

I thought about all the years of cultivating trust with my children and how even now my teenagers will come plop on my bed to discuss life or express needs. If I hadn't spent their whole lives up until then showing up for them, connecting to them, or listening to them, this would not happen.

I look back to seasons where I have lost my way, listened to advice I knew wasn't best for my family, or questioned my instincts as a mother, and they are definitely marked with difficulty and frustration. Trying to be like friends we only view on social media, trying to fit children into the molds of their siblings, trying to fit ourselves into molds of what a good parent is, this all leads to disconnection and dissatisfaction.

So, keep up the work in your own self so that when you need to find your way again, you don't have to look for an expert, because you are the expert in your own child.

6

Choose your battles so the important stuff can be heard

I remember waking up when I had a 2-year-old and not wanting to get out of bed because I knew the day was going to be a war zone. It wasn't just a possibility; it was a guarantee that much of my day would be tied up in mini battles. I wanted so badly to raise a good kid that I went against my go-with-the-flow nature and was hyper vigilant of my son's behavior; I was quick to deal with anything even remotely amiss. This hyper awareness was intense at home, but it got worse around other people...playdates, being around grandparents, the check out at the grocery store when the sweet older lady behind me was watching with a raised eyebrow. I often felt like I was on trial and I didn't want to fail. To be honest, it had little to do with him, but a lot to do with me, with wanting to be thought of in a good light. I heard the whispers sometimes, *I would never let my kid talk to me that way*, or from a grandparent, *I certainly would not have let you get away with that when you were his age*. I felt like I was in defense mode all the time, in a constant state of fight or flight and it felt terrible. I cannot imagine what it was like for him, a two-year-old just trying to learn and grow.

Just imagine this: you're an adult at your job, but you're around someone who watches your every move and criticizes it or tries to modify your behavior all day long. Not fun and honestly not conducive of being your best self. In the end, I think a lot of my discipline for my son became white noise to him and because of this he often didn't even hear me. It was maddening.

I remember this one time so vividly, I had a house guest who made it known that she didn't approve of my parenting, or my child. The misery of hosting while being sleep deprived from waking up with his newborn brother, while trying to nip every potential misbehavior in the bud was exhausting. First thing in the morning my son wanted a green sippy cup to drink his milk out of. That particular sippy cup was dirty so I poured it into a perfectly fine blue cup and was sure to let him know he was going to have to get over his disappointment. For hours he cried about it. The more he cried, the more I dug my heels in as I sweated under the skeptical eyes of disapproval.

It was torture. Deep down I knew that if she wasn't there, I would have washed the green cup and gone about our day. After all, to me, the mom, it didn't matter what color cup he drank his milk out of and it was just not a battle worth fighting.

If I could go back, I would *let so much go*. Instead of putting my foot down about eating all of his sandwich, I would let it go so when I needed to teach him something important, like not running into the road, he heard me. Instead of forcing him to wear something I wanted him to wear, I would let it go and save my precious breath to talk to him about ways to play nicely with a friend in the sandbox.

We all only have so much energy and our children have only so much attention.

By the time my son was 5 I started letting go of stuff that

didn't matter. I think part of it was exhaustion and part of it was just time, space, and perspective. Living life on a battlefield was unsustainable. Alone at our house it was easy to ignore the little things, but being out in public it still felt so hard. I was defensive about my choices to not fight certain battles, but it was worth it for the peace we started experiencing for longer periods of time. Because my instructions weren't constant, he was actually able to hear me for the important things. Our days became much more enjoyable and even fun. So what if he wanted to go outside without a coat on or wear a superhero cape to church? I loved not having to fight about every single thing.

Now that little 2-year-old is a teenager and I still find myself slowing down and checking in before entering into any sort of battle. I'm not going to nitpick about a few curse words he's listening to in a song because for me, I would rather spend my time chatting about his relationships or listening to him talk about being offered drugs in the locker room. Someone else might choose to fight that battle but it's not the most important thing to me.

Choosing battles is often about putting up blinders for how everyone else is doing it and honing in on that intuition about what is important to your family. It's about knowing your child, knowing yourself, and figuring out what you want to spend your energy on. I highly value creating space for conversation, so biting my tongue about something small that bothers me is worth it if it means that a car ride ends up being a time to chat and connect.

So, make a list of your priorities, keeping in mind that every family is different.

I let things like using curse words or not making their bed go. Instead, I want to use my words and energy to guide my children to empathy with other humans. Rather than eating their entire dinner, I focus on helping them listen to their own body when it comes to food. Instead of perfect grades, I want them to be curious about learning.

I bet if we surveyed the happiest adults, ones that love being in their job and have meaningful friendships, what they share in common would not be that their parents never let up on the discipline. You cannot force children to be good adults by the sheer will of correction.

In the end, our children are not going to be made by being forced to wear itchy sweaters, not eating their lunch, or accidentally being too loud at the library. So, keep to the important stuff.

7

Kids have bad days too

I'm used to not fitting in. I had a very sheltered childhood. I didn't watch TV growing up so I know nothing about pop culture or cartoons that my peers watched on Saturday mornings. I find myself feeling excluded when a group of my peers get nostalgic about the 80's and 90's. Feeling left out of pop culture is not all of it. I also find myself in my lat 30's now, feeling crippled about saying how I feel—allowing myself to have a wide range of emotions without shame. I view my peers and the way they navigate life and I can't help but feel like I missed out on something. I think back to many occasions when I was feeling sad or lonely as a little girl and most of these memories end in me hiding. One vivid memory I have is being left out of a game with my cousin and hiding under my bed for hours, sobbing and crying because my heart hurt so badly. I didn't live in a home where this kind of feeling was allowed, so I learned to hide and act bravely early on.

Well into my journey as a parent, I started allowing myself to have bad days out loud for the first time in my life. Even as I awkwardly relearned these basics it still wasn't until my oldest was 10 years old that I had the realization that he was a full human too and should be allowed to have bad days. I don't know why! I guess I just got so focused on raising him, meeting his needs, and guiding him, that I forgot that he was like me, like everyone else on the planet.

This realization came about one day when I was talking to a friend about some challenges from the day before.

"Yeah, kids are humans. . .they have bad days too."

I was speechless. I had never thought about it like that. She was right.

I thought about my quite often bad days and how I needed to be supported through them and immediately my heart sank. I had not been allowing my kids to have bad days. I had been punishing them for every bad attitude, I had made mountains out of mole hills if I saw any kind of outburst, and yet I had bad days and outbursts and expected sympathy and grace when it came to me.

Bad days don't mean you're a bad parent. Bad days don't mean that your kids will be a bad adult. Bad days happen to everyone and everyone deserves to feel safe to have them.

At the time I realized this I had a 10 year old, an 8 year old, and a 5 year old and I felt like I had ruined them by not realizing this sooner. I thought of so many days that ended in long arguments and time-outs that probably simply started because of a bad day.

I started asking questions before jumping to punishment for an outburst.

"How are things with your friends?"

"How is school?"

Often I found out these little humans had experienced something hard in their little worlds and because they haven't learned how to communicate complex feelings they cried, lashed out, or caused trouble because of it.

I started viewing them as I would a friend coming home

from a long, frustrating day at work, and the results of this have been staggering. Instead of being in a head-to-head battle for hours, there is a softening: a little extra coziness, a tea and a head scratch, a quick little trip for a late-night milkshake, an extra hour of screen time to watch a movie. Support instead of judgment.

Today I have two teenagers and a tween who is starting to change in her hormones and there are a lot of bad days in this house.

Just a few months ago one of my teenagers was fighting with his brother and being out-of-character-rude to me. I grounded him immediately. His anger got worse and he told me "I don't care." My initial reaction was to ground him more to prove that he did in fact care. My mind was racing. *He can't act like this; he'll be a terrible man one day if I let him get away with this.* But a small voice told me to stop what I was doing and listen to him. I finally got him away from the other kids and just sat with him, awkwardly at first. It took 25 minutes for him to open up and then the tears came. He ran outside in the winter cold in just shorts and came back with red and wet eyes, embarrassed. Turns out his best friend of 3 years had stopped talking to him, he was lonely, and there was a rumor going around school about him.

Here he was, a popular kid with lots of friends; it seemed to me that he had it all and certainly he didn't have problems like me, an adult with REAL problems. But in his world, things were really hard. He was experiencing a lot of grief that was masking as impatience and anger. He was having the worst day. That shift in how I dealt with him made such a difference. He softened, he was allowed to feel the feelings, and the atmosphere of the entire home shifted with him.

Even though shifting this perspective has been profound, I so easily forget. Our society is so performance driven, we don't value rest, and I so quickly get in that groove of trying to move my children through our days with the goal of "being good" or "doing good". Sometimes the bad days sneak up on me and it's when I am in the midst of a frustrating argument that I have to pause and take a few steps back. Bad days are allowed in our house and are usually met with a little extra love. Viewing bad days as what they are, naming them, and having grace for them allows for many more good days to come.

8

When things feel really hard, get outside

It was just one of those days when it feels like everything is hard. My kids were bickering in that particular tone that just grates on my last nerve, the dishes had overtaken the sink, nothing on my "to do list" had gotten checked off, and I had no plans for dinner. In that moment I really, really wished I wasn't a stay-at-home parent. I let my mind fantasize about getting take out and eating dripping hot noodles in front of my television with absolutely no other noises. I remember standing in the kitchen, mind muddy, hair pulled up into a top knot of tangles, and deciding we were going to turn this day around. I grabbed the kids and a few diapers, jumped in the car, and started driving. I turned on music and slowly but surely the bickering melted away into humming and laughing. I swung by a fast-food joint, grabbed two bags full of food that hopefully someone would find tasty, and I found myself parked by a river with roots to climb on and rocks to skip. As I unloaded the kiddos, my heart rate was still high and I felt so frayed at the edges. I sat down in the dirt and started to cry silently. This was SO hard; this was such a hard day. I didn't feel like I was cut out for this motherhood thing.

Just a few minutes into my cry everything changed. In a complete 180 turn I had come to a place where my nervous system was regulated and their nervous systems were regulated. Suddenly the muddiness of my brain cleared and I was able to cope. And not just cope! I was actually enjoying that little end to our day. We got home that night dirty and happy.

Kids have a lot of energy. Go to a trampoline park on a rainy day and observe the seemingly unending bouncing and flipping. I think that a lot of the usual frustrations of parenthood stem from the mismatched balance of energy between us and them. Just check in with a parent on the second day of being snowed in and you will *feel* it.

Children need to run, to push themselves, to explore, to try new things. And unfortunately, our society is set up so that children do not even almost get enough of this. One hour playground trips and recess at school will not meet this need. But goodness, we parents are so exhausted and many of us are dealing with mental health struggles like anxiety or depression and the thought of loading up the car with the snacks and extra outfits (just in case) can sometimes feel so daunting that we opt for staying home or staying inside where it seems much more manageable. But it rarely is. After a few hours of staying inside, by the time dinner rolls around, parents are frustrated and kids are antsy.

Just 50 years ago children were outside for hours a day building forts, problem solving, interacting face-to-face with other children, and falling asleep tired. Nowadays children are on screens for hours, obesity is at an all time high, depression and anxiety are rampant, and kids feel alone, incapable, and lethargic. We have to dose them with melatonin to get them to sleep at night, we have to dose them to sit still during school, we have to dose them to keep their insulin in check.

One random freezing cold day in the winter, I went down a rabbit hole researching how Scandinavian cultures deal with their long and dark winter days. I was shocked to read that every single day, no matter how cold it was, children are dressed to play outside and even young babies nap every day in the bitter cold, all bundled up. Their children are statistically happier and healthier than children in the United States.

As our green spaces have become harder to get to and our neighborhoods have become harder to play in and our children are suffering. Being outside, problem solving, running till they can't anymore, climbing trees, and noticing the beauty in nature should not be a privilege only afforded to families with time and money, but it feels like it is.

So, on days when you want to jump ship because you're tired and your children are not. GET OUTSIDE at any cost! Research and find public places, community places—the creek off the side of the road, a community garden, people who want the same for their children. Let go of making every outing idyllic, be ok with dirt, let them try something that seems too hard for them.

Yes, you'll have more laundry, but I guarantee everyone will sleep better at night.

Ideas for when you're outside

- Bring a large bowl and a spoon. Let them make a soup with water, dirt, leaves, flowers, and pieces of bark. You will need to pretend to taste it.
- Bring an old sheet and clothes pins to let them build a fort.
- Skip rocks.
- Give them a notebook to tape flowers and leaves in.
- Ask them to name different flowers and trees. My children renamed the trees that bloom pink in the spring "love trees" and we would shake them so it snowed.
- Find shapes in the clouds.
- Give them a long rope, you'd be surprised at the things they can do with it.
- Learn to make a little fire together.
- Roll down hills.
- Start a rock collection.
- Encourage them to climb trees.
- Go "exploring" by letting them lead you off of paths and let them discover new places.

9

You need a village and a village is built by you showing up

It was just a random Tuesday. A random Tuesday where everyone was too hot, too tired, and our own small homes felt too small. And so friends gathered in my little backyard around dinner time. One family brought half of a rotisserie chicken, one person stopped at the grocery store on the way over and grabbed chips and salsa and a giant tub of watermelon. I made peanut butter and jelly sandwiches. Adults sat on the porch and kids ran around and climbed the old play set I had gotten for free from a neighbor. No one was hosting, no one was performing, and there was such a sense of peace as we allowed our village to come into our lives.

There is a well-known quote that says "it takes a village to raise a child". I would like to offer an alternate way to say it: Raising a child without a village is freaking hard.

Lately I've been seeing a lot of memes making fun of the whole village concept. They say,

"Where is my village?" or "Still waiting on that village."

Here's the brutal truth of it all—villages don't just happen in the world today; *you* have to make your village. It starts with you.

Our society has become so individualized, so shut off from the outside world that you actually have to do some work to get your village and many people do not do that work. That work is scary and foreign. Rejection feels imminent but in reality, so many people are in the same lonely boat wishing for community and support.

When I was raising babies, I had a wonderful community surrounding me. I did attend a church at that time and my kids attended preschool which gave me weekly exposure to people outside of my family, but that was not enough. I often heard remarks about how lucky I was, or how jealous someone was of my village. While I did surround myself with incredible humans who I learned a lot from and who showed up for me and I them, I don't think it's because I found the right people necessarily. I truly believe that anyone can develop their own community. But if you wait for it to come to you, you will be waiting forever. It's not just about putting yourself in situations where there are other people (i.e. a baby music class, a playground in your neighborhood); it's about inviting people into your world. Maybe this looks like taking small talk to a deeper level, being curious about someone else, or inviting someone into your home. At its very core, community is really about inviting people into our messy lives and breaking down the false walls we have built to protect us.

I had a friend one time that told me she really wanted to be friends with another mom that she had met at the library. They had *tried* to get together for SIX MONTHS. Anxiety, fear, and anticipation had them both canceling for every runny nose. Once it was even because one of them hadn't had a chance to clean. In that situation someone needed to make the first move, the first outreach to say, "I'm not perfect, but I need connection." That in turn gives permission for others to do that as well.

One of my very fondest memories in those bleary first years of parenthood was when a dear friend stopped by to chat. My house was in disarray, I hadn't showered in 2 days, and all I had to offer her was coffee and cauliflower. We ended up sitting on my dirty kitchen floor and having the best conversation while our children ran around like feral cats. When she left, I felt so encouraged, seen, and loved. I didn't feel alone. I think about it all the time; if I had felt the need to "have it together" that day I would have missed out on what I desperately needed.

We do not need perfection to have connection.

I cannot do it all is a common sentiment from parents. And to that I say—yeah you can't, because we aren't meant to do it all. We are meant to live in community, not holed up in our homes bearing all the burdens, meeting all the needs. We need others. So however you need to get there, start gathering your village. Host a last-minute scrap dinner by texting people, "Want to bring your leftovers over?" Maybe the lasagna you might be sick of will be just the thing for someone else. Let other people invest in your children, celebrate when your friend's child takes their first steps, multiply the love. I promise you, when people gather in a way that is real, magic will happen. And then as you build trust you can all share in the staggering calling of raising children.

I once knew a group of women who would take turns each week helping one of them deep clean their home. It became a time to crank up the 90s music, laugh, and get the boring stuff done. They would rotate each week.

Maybe you don't have a messy life. Maybe your life is incredibly put together. I have this incredible friend who has an absolute gift of keeping a cozy and clean home. She also relishes to feed people delicious, made from scratch food when they are over. This isn't to impress me and I can feel that after being in her home for 10 minutes. She has told me that she struggles sometimes with loneliness as people sometimes make comments about how together she was and draw a line between her and them. People don't like feeling like they aren't measuring up—but when I allowed myself to show up in her home and just *be* I was able to receive the gift of her friendship.

Villages are built through:

Vulnerability
Honesty
Flexibility
Simplicity
And showing up.

Don't be afraid. Take that first step. Your village needs you, and you need them.

10

What a child needs to feel satisfied is your presence

I had so much to do that day. Two meals worth of dishes were waiting for me in the sink, work that was past due, and 4 loads of laundry sitting on the couch. Little 4-year-old hands were tugging at my skirt and "Mama! Mama!" was a constant soundtrack to the morning. I didn't have time to play. Maybe because it felt like the productivity of that day was already a bust, or maybe the 78th "Mama" broke me but I stopped what I was doing and grabbed some Lego Duplos to build a tower with my son. That first step of stopping felt so hard but once I was sitting cross legged on the hardwood floor, locking eyes with his sparkly ones, and hearing his imaginative interpretation of how his little Transformer toy would scale the wall we were building—it felt like this was actually the most important thing to do that day.

I'm a highly imaginative person, I always have been. My childhood was jam packed with playing pretend for hours with my sisters and cousins. We made soup from pine needles and grass, rescued each other from giants, and played dress up for tea parties.

I have the fondest memories of those days, so it was really interesting to find out when I became a mother that playing with my own kids regularly did not come naturally. I would end up feeling like I was sitting there, listening to a small dictator boss me around while my mile long list of things I could be accomplishing rotated in my head. I could never seem to play the right way and time just hung in limbo.

Then the preschool my children attended did a class on child-led play and I learned two things:

1. It is very, very important to play with your children

2. I was doing it wrong

It wasn't anything earth shattering, it was simply letting my child tell me what to do, asking questions like "Oh where should the horse go next?" or "What should my name be?" I didn't offer my ideas; I was just near and present.

It was too simple, but it worked. My needy child who had been pestering me to play was completely satiated after just 10 minutes and all I had to do was put aside my desire to contribute to the play.

This lesson translated to many other aspects of my parenting journey, drilling into my head that quality was valued over quantity. Instead of looking at the day ahead as one long play date, I would give undivided attention for less than half an hour, putting my phone away and making eye contact. Soon the play felt less tiresome. I started enjoying the click of Legos or Transformers and the babble of whatever was in that child's imagination. Every few minutes I would exclaim "Wow!" or "Interesting!" and marvel at how they always responded so positively to it.

I have struggled my whole life with bouts of depression related to Bipolar Disorder and it didn't stop when I became a mother. I had to get creative when basic life skills felt like mountains. Through it all I really had to dig deep for the simplest ways to be present with my children: laying under the Christmas tree to look at the lights, cuddling on a rainy day, or eating our lunch outside and leaving my phone inside. It's no doubt that mental illness has stolen from my children but it has been incredible to hear what memories they treasure from when they were little. It wasn't the big things like the one day we went to Disney or the expensive movie dates. It is those small reaches, the ones in which pretty much all I could offer was my brief presence that they love: draping a blanket over our dining room table and reading to them, playing with dolls, pretending to check out at a grocery store with an old calculator. Years later, I went through a really awful divorce. 17 years of a very toxic marriage had reduced me to a shell of myself and I was bedridden with depression. The thought of losing my children to half-time custody felt like the worst thing ever, which was a big part of why I stayed for so long. The minute I got brave and left the marriage, I started to come to life. It was obvious after a week that me being present and healthy 50% of the time was vastly better than me barely functioning for every waking moment.

Think back to your own childhood and what stands out. My father says his favorite memory of his dad was sitting on the floor and rolling a ball between them. When he talks about it, he tears up and his eyes sparkle. My mother's favorite memory of her father is piling blankets in the back of their station wagon for long trips. My own memories of my parents are complicated and sometimes painful, but they are sprinkled with simple, good memories that I will never forget and which bring such warm feelings to me. Memories like my dad, dirty from work, leaning over a cup of diner coffee with me and a game of clue. Or flattening an old box so we could slide down the steep hill near our house. There was that time my mom woke me up in the dark for a surprise bike ride to watch the sunrise over an old, green Stanley thermos of hot cocoa and the time she built a snowman with me.

Kids don't want the fancy stuff; they don't want you to substitute time with you with things. So put down your phone, shelf your to do list, and spend 10 good minutes immersed in their world. Grab a kid for your grocery shopping trip where they get to choose the music for the ride and maybe pick out a pack of gum. Be silly and dance when you feel like you don't have a moment to spare. If your children are older, take a few minutes to research a subject they're interested in so you have something to chat about.

I promise you; you'll be surprised how *enough* it will be.

11

You cannot have perfect days every day

I can vividly imagine a perfect life and it haunts me. A life where I wake up rested, float down the stairs in my fresh cotton nightgown to make breakfast for my family. Where everything is in its place, my children are happy, there's no fighting, I am able to work from home, and we all gather for the kind of dinner that could grace a magazine cover. I am reminded about 15 minutes into every day that I am not that mom, and frankly, I don't know anyone who is that mom.

We can't do all the things all the time. We just can't.

Some days I manage to cook yummy, healthy, well-balanced meals, but those days aren't the days that I play on my belly on the ground with my kids. The days I get them to bed at a decent hour aren't the days that I let them explore in nature for hours.

I had a pediatrician tell me something once and it has stuck with me ever since. My young child had gone through a period of time where, despite having always eaten a wide variety of food, he had started being very picky. I was worried he wasn't getting a well-balanced diet. As a first-time parent I was wrecked with guilt and concerned for his long-term health. I felt like a terrible mother.

After hearing my concerns he said, "As long as he's getting a balanced diet in a 2 week time block, that's ok. He doesn't need to consume a perfect diet every day."

That might make a nutritionist cringe, but it gave me so much flexibility and changed the way I viewed things. It took the pressure off.

I started viewing other things this way. I can have a bedtime routine and I can also go on a date night or take a last-minute adventure. It doesn't mean that my child will never go to sleep on time. Maybe one day I need to get a lot done and they watch more TV than usual, it doesn't mean that is our normal.

As I wove in and out of busy days, working, staying home, figuring things out I felt free to let go of the reins sometimes. Veggies were snuck into spaghetti sauce and one day the picky period sort of lifted. I mostly kept to a low screen time when they were young, and I didn't feel derailed if I indulged in back-to-back movies when I needed a rest.

I will admit, I am a free-spirited sort, so this shift was an easy one for me. Inevitably we would live in a state of flexibility, solely based on the way I am made up. But letting go of the of trying to have a perfect day, allowed me grace for myself; it allowed me to not live in constant guilt and dread.

For my type-A friends who struggle with flexibility, not having the goal of having a perfect day every day is really hard to let go of. They will end up having more days that check all of the boxes than I will, but they have told me how much they wish they could let loose of the reins once in a while.

Parenting this way has really helped shape my children

into well-rounded humans who can adjust when the inevitable twist in the road happens. It has allowed me to stand back and look at the big picture more. This type of approach allows room for the best parts of life to unfold, and the parts of life you will fondly remember in your old age.

12

Look at mistakes as tools not failures

I found out recently that one of my teenagers said something inappropriate to one of their friends, and a mom had overheard. Teenagers, with their undeveloped brains and their pension for shock value sometimes do this. From the outside I can see their awkwardness as they push and test boundaries. It didn't mean I wasn't embarrassed and horrified. It didn't mean I didn't sit down with him and have a big, serious talk. The mother I was 10 years ago would have absolutely fallen apart in this situation. I would have blamed myself; I would have tightened up on discipline and grounded him for eternity. Instead, I sat with him and asked questions. *Why did he say that? Did he think that was appropriate? What if someone had said that to his grandmother?* And then I told him that even if you don't mean it, words are powerful and can destroy people and reputations in an instant. And that was that. As much as I wish it didn't happen, I hope that he carries that little lesson with him as he navigates his life. I hope it will save him from pain in the long run.

As a brand-new parent, I started out with a false sense of control that has gradually lessened the older I get. Not only do I see it in my own parenting, but in observing other families around me. Some of the very best parents I know have kids who make not so great decisions. Some of the very best people I know come from not so great home lives. Even if I was the first perfect parent in the history of the world, that would not guarantee that my child would turn out the way I wanted them to.

Once I realized this, I felt initial panic, and then I felt so much relief. It took a little bit of time and it wasn't until the teen years that my thoughts on parenting sort of solidified.

CHILDREN DON'T NEED ME TO TELL THEM WHAT TO DO—THEY NEED ME TO HELP THEM GAIN TOOLS FOR THEIR LIVES.

Thinking back on my childhood, I remember having absolute paralysis from fear of making a mistake or choosing the wrong thing. One time I prayed for an entire week because I didn't know if God wanted me to go to see *Pearl Harbor* with friends when I was 17, because it was rated R. While I was behaving and people pleasing, my peers were messing up, learning, moving on, and knowing better. I really entered my adult years with zero tools, except how to pretend to be good. In my late thirties I found myself making the same mistakes that my friends had made in high school. I longed for a redo on how I was raised and for the freedom to explore and figure things out before the stakes as a mother and adult were so much higher.

As I started gathering my own tools, my perspective changed. I started viewing mistakes my children made as opportunities for them to gain tools for their lives instead of just looking at it as a failure. I let natural consequences happen, even though it hurts to ever see them stumble. I stopped protecting them so damn much. I stopped parenting with the goal of them doing everything right, of making me look good as as parent.

I smile sometimes as I watch them live their lives. I feel comfort in the fact that they have the freedom to figure things out, to not do everything right, to learn from challenges. I feel good about where they are headed and I feel like I can breathe knowing that current pain, loss, or failure will ultimately help them prepare for the rest of their lives.

13

Ritual isn't a cage, it's an anchor

I love my birthday. I grew up the oldest of 7 children but on my birthday, I was queen. I got to pick what we ate for all three meals, I wore a flimsy silver crown all day, and at dinner everyone around the table would take turns saying what they loved about me. I loved knowing that no matter what, come October 12th, that year would be marked with celebration. Holidays growing up were always very marked with tradition. I knew what to expect. I looked forward to the ritual of welcoming Christmas, the first day of school, or eating green grits on St Patrick's Day.

While those seasonal rhythms felt wonderful, I grew up with very few daily rhythms. My dad moved every few months for his job and the way my days unfolded changed so often. While many children were doing their Tuesday chores, I was crossing the country in our green van or getting to a motel in Arizona at 2 am. Even though there were challenges, I really did enjoy the way I grew up. It was exciting and we had experiences that people only dream about. As an adult, looking back, I do see how rhythm is a very important skill that will over time give stability, security, and a less frantic day-to-day. My mother did have one daily ritual she held tight to no matter what, and that was gathering us to read us chapter books every single night. That practice absolutely was the heartbeat of my childhood and I look back on it with a lot of nostalgia.

While many people I know would loosen up and break the daily monotony of living if they could go back, my number one regret in raising my children is that I did not adhere to very much ritual during our early days and seasons.

I have struggled as an adult to not live in utter chaos all the time. The way I grew up gave me some incredible memories, many of my friends envy my ease to divert from plans or drop anything for something fun, but in reality, my children and family suffered greatly with the unpredictability and the mess that resulted from not valuing any sort of routine.

I love being a free spirit. I love being spontaneous. The thought of forcing myself into a strict routine feels stifling, but I wish I had been able to step back and instead of thinking I had to be rigid, seeing opportunities to weave in moments of ritual to anchor us all. I know it would have made me a better mother; it would have given me some much needed peace and given my children some parameters that felt less frustrating as they always wondered what was next.

Maybe you struggle with routine like me or maybe being rigid feels like a security blanket and you don't know how to get out from under the strict boundaries you've put up. Either way, taking the time to step back, evaluate, and maybe rearrange how you think about your long days of parenting can be so valuable.

I had this one beautiful season with my three that naturally fell into a little midday ritual and I really treasure those months. I made the decision to let my son ride the bus home from first grade so that my daughter Lucy could nap uninterrupted. During that sacred part of the day my middle son, who was so chill he often fell through the cracks, would help me prep or cook dinner. We put on music and it was SO therapeutic to us all. Not only did I get that special one-on-one time with him, it was such an anchor before the witching hour of tired kids, tired mama, and their daddy coming home from work.

I've never been one to do an elaborate bedtime routine. As an introvert and highly sensitive person, I was always at my wit's end when bedtime came around. For years I would put them to bed abruptly, desperate for those few hours of quiet that revived my soul. I took note of my peers and their lavender baths, 3 book rule, and multiple songs and I felt good about my choice to just do it quickly. Yes, I would rock them as babies, and if they were having a particularly hard day I would cuddle up and sing to them, but it wasn't every night and nothing was set in stone. Doing bedtime this way made it easier to get a babysitter for a date night or for them to have a grandparent take care of them. Generally, I've felt ok about our lack of routine at night, but fast forward to my youngest being 10—splitting time between two households and her anxiety about "what was next" made me realize I might need to reevaluate. I realized I needed to implement a lot of ritual on the nights I had her so that she felt calm; warm tea, chatting for 10 minutes, sharing a song, and then holding her tight and long. It has come to be a sweet time. I'm not as tired physically as I once was and I'm able to be present most nights. If I could go back, I would not be so extreme. Maybe a one hour bedtime routine wasn't for me, but there could absolutely have been a balance of a quick little routine to make us all feel like we could wrap up our days calmly. I have come to view ritual as a little gift instead of a cage, a place to implement celebration, not just a feeling of drudgery. And ritual isn't just meant for our days, it can be implemented in seasons, birthdays, and holidays. Something as simple as a Valentine's banner and heart-shaped pancakes every February, or choosing the dinner menu on your birthday can absolutely inject joy into these lives we live.

This winter I took a course by Johanna Holmgren entitled *A Guide to Creating a Seasonal Family Rhythm* (you need to check it out). and I immediately felt tears running down my face on the first paragraph because it felt too late for me. After all, I had a high schooler who sometimes got home at 10 pm from away sports games and I didn't even have my children every day. Her course absolutely lit a fire in me to take little opportunities now, that it wasn't too late. We started what we call "Family Time" any time we could. I gathered a container with paper and pens, and a basket with cozy blankets. We all put our devices away and one kid was in charge of the music we played. For 15 minutes we talk, doodle, and cuddled up. We absolutely cannot keep it up every day of the week, but when I start feeling disconnected or like we are flying through space, it anchors us. I hope that they remember these brief times like I do of my mama reading to me at night, as these are the anchors that hold the ship from keeling over.

14

Let your kids be bored

I loved the attic of my first home. The creaky ladder that got pulled down felt like the portal to endless possibilities. When I crested the top of the last rung, I was always hit with a wall of hot, stale air and still to this day that particular smell takes me right back to my childhood. In this attic I was left alone for hours with my sisters to play. There was no orchestration of what we were to play by my mother, there were no new toys, it was just us and our imaginations. Certain dark corners became new worlds to discover, old pieces of wood became furniture, and my grandmother's old scarves became cloaks. There was even one time we nearly burnt the whole house down by drying our socks on the old lamp we used.

I don't know when exactly parents being in charge of entertaining their children 24/7 became a thing, but it absolutely is in a lot of households. Screen time is off the charts, companies make millions offering educational toys, and fidgets fill every waking moment with stimulation. Being a photographer and doula, I find myself in different homes and I notice a lot of hands-on interaction with babies and young children to the point I feel like there is absolutely no downtime. Parents are exhausted and children are overstimulated. For a while there was a term helicopter parent that was coined to describe someone hovering and protecting their child at every possible moment. You can spot these people on a playground, and it brings me anxiety to watch them. Of course we want to connect with our kids, to keep them safe, to protect them from scraping their knee or breaking a bone, but I also think that leaving kids alone to play, to figure things out, to push their bodies is INVALUABLE. And I think it is becoming a lost art. Boredom is the catalyst to creativity. It is the place that tools for navigating life grow. If you hover over your child and force making friends on the playground, it takes away from their ability to do it themselves. Waiting patiently in the wings as they stumble around or try something new is hard, but once you get in the habit, there comes a point that it will start to come naturally.

Most of us cannot just let our kids out the front door to run wild until dinner like our parents did with us. But we can leave out baskets of art supplies that can be pulled out, we can take them into nature with a bucket and a spoon for digging, we can let them create play out of anything they want.

I have this rule in my home that I will ALWAYS buy art supplies. To me, it is as necessary as food. I have several places throughout the house where it's ok to make a mess, to try something out. I often give my kids old boxes or bottles for them to create little inventions. Once one of my children spent an entire month creating a world of animals and documented all of it on lined notebook paper that he stapled and glued into a book. Another child tried to make a parachute. Yes, I knew he would never fly, but what he created out of the boredom I allowed to occur gave him the courage to always try new things.

When I was 8, I was learning about how trees and plants gave off oxygen. I was so transfixed by the idea of being able to scuba dive in the lake near my house that I planted some small plants inside of an empty coke bottle and taped a tube to a makeshift mask. My mother could have told me no, she could have put me in front of a TV to avoid a mess, but no, she encouraged me to try. That little lesson has stuck with me my whole life. I have a printed photo of me in my desk with my little invention, reminding me to not be afraid to try.

Having teenagers now I still fight this feeling of having to entertain them every day. First of all, I do not have the money to keep teenagers "happy". Compared to their peers we can not even do 10% of the trampoline parks or movies it feels like their friends are always going to. I am always observing from the sidelines and I have to say, I think even though my kids might complain once in a while about not having a constant stream of things to do, that they are generally happier than most of the kids their age. They can find beauty from sitting by the fire, taking a walk, or catching fireflies.

Of all the things to worry about in this life, take boredom off of your list.

15

Knowing life is made up of seasons allows you to enjoy it more

Spring makes me ache a little bit. The earth is transitioning to a new season, one that every human on earth welcomes after the harshness of winter. Spring also reminds me of my children being little and the long walks I would take with them before dinner. Walking with little ones makes me see details I might usually miss. Even though we only walked a mile or so, those miles were magical. We helped worms from the sidewalk to the grass, we oooh and ahhhed at the new flowers, and we shook the weeping cherry tree till it snowed pink all around us. The warmth of spring brings back that magic. . .it also brings back the bone deep weariness that comes from parenting young kids. And so I don't even wish to be back there. I smile softly and let that feeling of nostalgia wash over me, and I return to the season I'm in now in. A season in which I sleep all night, don't have to wipe anyone else's bottom, and stay up late talking about life with my partner.

Those well-meaning ladies at the checkout line telling you that it goes too fast and to enjoy it, they obviously mean well. Like I said earlier, it doesn't help to hear that when you're in the thick of it, when you are so exhausted that you fantasize about getting into a tiny accident so you could rest in a hospital for a day. But what they really are trying to tell you is that this season you are in will not last. This is heartbreaking when it comes to things like toddler babble, nursing babies, or those months where they wore a superhero cape for months on end. But it also means that the parts that are hard will not be hard forever, and this is something we will need to remind each other of.

My first child was raring to go at 5 am or earlier every single morning for years and years. I am not a morning person and it was incredibly hard to adjust to. Actually, come to think of it, I don't know that I ever did. People with teenagers would tell me with love that it was just a season and that one day I would have to wake *him* up on weekends. I truly thought that I would be the first person in the world to never have their child sleep in, but I clung to that hope that it wouldn't always be like this. They were right. My children now sleep in, all of them. They make their own breakfast and suddenly I'm given the gift of my slower mornings again.

Each and every season, just like the ones that mark summer, fall, winter, and spring, also give gifts. In the winter it is the fact that you have to slow down, by the time spring comes to warm we are greeted with flowers wherever you look, summer brings opportunity for adventure and a break from school or work, and about the time the summer heat has drained all your energy, the crisp air of fall fills your lungs.

I always tell my tired families that I work with who have energetic toddlers,

"God made them cute to survive."

I say it with a smile and wink, but it's true! There are so many dear things that come alongside the physical exhaustion in the first years. Thank goodness we don't have to do it forever, but at least when we are doing it, we can giggle at the funny things they say or get lost in their loving gaze.

As they grow and the physical demands lessen, we might find ourselves having to deal with more parenting decisions and complex emotions.

I love the quote from Emily Dickinson, "That it will never come again is what makes life so sweet."

It is so true. The ebb and flow of life is what makes life so precious.

We can make it through these seasons knowing the hard parts will change and pass—so we can treasure up the good parts. Nothing lasts forever.

16

You don't have to MAKE memories, they just happen

Nostalgia is a powerful thing. The fact that random memories can be triggered by smells, sounds, tastes, or places is truly a beautiful part of being human. There is a certain salty smell I equate to my Aunt Lucy's beach house and one whiff of something similar reminds me of love and dancing barefoot to music from the 1940's. The song "Silent Night" instantly brings me a feeling of belonging as I remembered playing violin on the stage at church every Christmas and looking out into the congregation at the illuminated faces of people I loved. The sound of a diesel truck reminds me of the way my heart would start racing when I knew my daddy was finally turning into our driveway on his way home from work. The old-fashioned Christmas cookie recipe passed down to me on a stained and crinkled note card brings back feelings of being a child and the magic of Christmas. I could eat an entire bowl of the dough and I relish every bite I take. However, it is confirmed by everyone else not in our family that they are, in fact, the worst cookie they've ever tasted. Pulling into the low country, with the giant oak trees and the Spanish moss that hangs like tinsel feels like home. These memories are just a scratch in the surface of the treasure trove I have of cherished times in my life. When I became a parent, I felt so much pressure to gift my children with their own nostalgic memories.

There are two times of year that absolutely exhaust me: Christmas and summer.

There is so much pressure to create memories for our children during these times of year. A quick browse of Pinterest can give you a million ideas on how to serve your kids watermelon shaped like a firecracker, crafts, adventures, recipes, activities, it never ends. And just when you think the bombardment of "better than" is over, Susie makes her kid's lunch a scene from *Land Before Time.*

Social media doesn't help the matter. One quick browse through Instagram and you feel like everyone else is doing things and you're just surviving. There are the families who hike every weekend, their children lined up like little ducks. The ones who manage to have their Christmas card, with matching jammies and hot cocoa in your mailbox the day after Thanksgiving. And Mother's and Father's Day crafts that you know will never grace your fridge.

I was always in a space of feeling like I wasn't doing enough. But according to whom? Certainly not according to my children.

I remember one particularly busy Christmas my kids begged me, "Can you just stop forcing this memory making?" They were exhausted and one more ornament craft was going to push them over the edge.

I was stunned. Didn't they see I was doing this for them?

But the thing is, me frantically forcing the memory making actually inhibited my kids from making their own authentic memories.

Every year after I put the Christmas tree ornaments away, I tuck a little handwritten note to myself in the top of the plastic bin. The first time I did it I reminded myself for the next year to not drink so much damn egg nog and to grocery shop before Christmas Eve because we have to eat even if there's a lot going on.

That year I just wrote: "Stop MAKING memories and BE in them."

I honestly still struggle. My romantic little self is always striving to create an atmosphere that will be beautifully nostalgic for them. My own memories that bring about warmth and a soft smile goad me on. Because it feels like if I let go of the control, they might not have these type of nostalgic memories when they are adults.

Being motivated in this way has caused a lot of tears and frustration. For years on end, my desire for a magical reading of *Twas the Night Before Christmas* like I had as a girl sent me into a tailspin of anger when they were wiggly or didn't want to wear their Christmas pj's.

If I could go back, I would let go from holding so tightly, trusting that memories are born in safe places. A parent pulling out their hair, because things didn't unfold like she envisioned, is not a safe place. I would allow my children to rest, to be. . .to find their way to what was important to them. I would log on to social media and say "good for them!" instead of "I need to be like them."

My children are half grown already. I am starting to notice their own nostalgia, the things that stick out to them. And I'm here to tell you, it's not anything I've created.

17

Quality over quantity when it comes to documenting your children

I have a box of old childhood photos that I break out every once in a while. I love scouring the background for glimpses of my old house or family members that have long since passed away. I laugh at my 90's style jumpers and uncomfortable Easter clothes. Pictures are powerful.

I've been a professional photographer for 20 years. I can't tell you how many hundreds of thousands of photos I have of my children stored in the cloud or on old computers or phones.

My children are just now enjoying seeing photos that they usually bemoaned me taking way back when. In fact, I'm delighted with the conversations these photos have sparked and hearing their own recollections of days I treasured.

I may not prioritize deep cleaning, but I do prioritize printing my photos. Our walls are a smattering of little moments that bring me back. Very little of them involve everyone smiling at the camera. When you first come into my home you are greeted with a giant black and white photo of just a normal afternoon. At 7, 5, and 2, my daughter is sporting a black eye and a fierce little smirk. Bare feet and mismatched clothes are the cherries on top.

I also have one wall in my house where I print photos off of my phone and tape them all together in an unorganized, but delightful, ode to how beautiful our life is.

Even though my home is filled with these photos, I STILL have yet to make any sort of album or baby book with the digital photos. So don't think I have it all figured out. Sometimes at night the sheer task of culling them, deciding what to add, and calculating the cost of printing so many albums keeps me frozen.

We all have to find what works for us and realize that doing something is better than doing nothing.

Is it overwhelming? Absolutely.

But we have to start somewhere.

HERE ARE my tips for capturing your children in a way that lasts:

- **Take videos.**

This is something I wish I had done more. No, I don't wish I had 200 more photos of their first birthday party, but yes, I wish I had 2 full minutes of their adorable chatter that didn't quite make sense.

- **Capture the mundane and the messy.**

Without a doubt, my favorite photos are not the ones with everyone in perfect outfits. They are the ones that showcase how things really were. As the years pass, and memories get fuzzy, you'll find that photos in the moment will become your most treasured possessions.

- **Balance being present and taking photos.**

With cell phones that have amazing cameras, it can be very easy to snap photos all the time when you're in a cool place or at a special event. I learned that when my kids were young that I was taking pictures all of the time and I wasn't even enjoying the times I was capturing. So, I kind of instituted a loose rule of choosing one day and one hour to take photos. We would go camping and I would keep my camera put up, enjoying s'mores with their sticky hands in mine, or swimming for hours in the creek. But I would decide one hour in which I would break it out and take photos of our camping trip.

Same for times like our beach trips. I would often leave my phone at the house we were renting and enjoy several days on the beach, just taking photos for an hour or so, usually the last days when our tans were brown and we had already spent a lot of time making memories.

- **Capture the weird things.**

I love going through my photos and remembering these little passing nuances that I had long since forgotten. The other day I was going way back 10 years on my Facebook memories and a photo popped up of Barclay with his pants tied to a chair. It triggered the best memory of the season that he was obsessed with knots and tied himself to everything. That worn tutu that you wish your 4-year-old would stop wearing? It will become so dear to you years from now. So, capture all those quirky little things.

- **Get in the photos.**

Do not rob your children of having you in their childhood photos. So what if you hate how your thighs look at the beach, or if you don't want to capture your aging wrinkles. Set a timer if you have to. Jump in the photos.

- **Cull them**

It is insane how many photos my phone holds. This is a blessing and a curse. I find that when I take, take, take photos that they get lost in the cloud and not enjoyed. So, taking the time to cull down to your very favorites will give you more opportunity to keep them safe, print them, or share them.

Quality over quantity.

- **Print them**

Don't think too hard. Don't plan too much. If you can't afford frames, tape them to your walls.

Start by ordering 50 photos right now off of your phone and see where you go from there. There are no rules, there are no comparisons. But waiting for perfection will keep you waiting forever.

- **Focus on how things feel, not how they look**

I always tell folks that I photograph for 10 years from now. Just know that your favorites will inevitably change as time robs you of the crispness of what it was like. Try focusing on how things felt instead of how they looked.

18

Life is not black and white, don't be afraid to venture into the gray

There had always been a line drawn between *them* and *me*. I was a normal person with a house and a family. I took a shower every day and wore shoes without holes in them. They were dirty, barefoot, and probably did things that caused their houseless-ness. They made bad choices; I made good ones.

And then one fall I found myself in a mixed episode of Bipolar Disorder and was admitted to the local psych ward for a few days. That distinction between them and me held steady for a few days. I hadn't known hunger so I picked at my lukewarm meal while they stole from the trays that went untouched. I called my family from the phone in the hall and they never had anyone answer. I lay in my bed thinking and they shook with symptoms of detox while doing laps around the nurses station for hours. And then I ventured out. Out of boredom I started chatting with people I would have otherwise put into a nice neat box of *others*. Turns out there was no line. It turns out that had I not had people in my life to step in when I wasn't well, that I would have 100% been in their position. That experience changed my life. It changed the way I look at people, at issues that rise up in this human experience. Now I look into the eyes of the houseless and smile at them. I rarely have cash but I acknowledge them as the worthy human beings that they are. I donate to local nonprofits that are helping get to the root of what is keeping them from housing or work. I support local places that come alongside addiction and change lives. And I no longer think that hard work always equals success.

I was raised with very black and white thinking in a very legalistic sect of Christianity. I was told what to believe and that much of life was either wrong or right. It seemed like every week everyone I knew would boycott an entire company because of values that didn't line up with ours. I didn't learn the tools of decision making or critical thinking until college and actually, mostly in my late thirties. I remember being in college and asking a friend if I was a Republican or a Democrat because I had always been told there was only one way to be if you loved Jesus.

Maybe you weren't raised like that, maybe you were given free rein to make your own decisions, maybe you wish you had been told what to think even for a few things— maybe that would have felt safer.

Something that has shifted as I have settled into my own knowing and have done work on my own story is that I no longer feel the need to tell my children what to believe or think. When we talk about issues that many people are polarized on, I love to have discussions with them. I want my children to figure out where they stand, not where their mother wants them to stand. I can tell them my thoughts on the matter, or share my own experiences or the experiences of others, but I no longer tell them what to believe or think.

I just want to talk about it.

Last year my ex called me really upset, "Are you telling our son you want him to have sex before marriage?"

I had to take some deep breaths so as not to fly off the handle. The trauma of being raised in purity culture and the harm it did to me as a woman and the harm I saw it have on my ex-husband bubbled up. Our son was in middle school at the time and sex didn't feel like it was even on his radar yet.

"Did I have a conversation with him about not marrying the first person he wanted to have sex with? Yes. Yes, I did."

It feels weird to parent without the rules I grew up with. It feels weird to take a back seat in being an expert in everything. Focusing on curiosity has helped me navigate this foreign pathway. Because the truth is that I do not have all the answers. The older I get, the less I see life in black and white. The more people that I get to know, I feel like I know less. I'm so glad my children will form their own opinions as they grow. I'm so glad that I'm modeling the art of asking questions, hearing different perspectives, LISTENING, and being able to change their mind without fear, as they gain more information. It's a skill I think many adults lack (just take a look around during election season).

There is much power in allowing yourself in the gray of life. Not only power, but empathy and compassion for other humans, which is what our world needs desperately.

19

Be open about the birds and the bees with your kids so that shame doesn't take root

I wouldn't wish my wedding night experience on anyone. I was a virgin and had been purposely sheltered from the evils of sex and my own body my whole life. But after a 20 minute ceremony and a 2 hour wedding reception I was supposed to bed my new husband in my carefully chosen white lacy nightgown. The only preparation I had done for the occasion was to read a Christian book that didn't even use the correct anatomical words and had more verses than advice. That night was awkward and a little traumatizing and it didn't get better for years. I remember being absolutely horrified that kids in high school were doing this weird and unnatural act. It took almost 2 decades for me to shed the shame I had developed regarding my body. Being dissociated from my body not only meant I was having really bad sex, but it meant that I allowed people to mistreat me, to hurt me, and to control me.

Most new parents hold their fresh new babies and think talking to that little one about anything to do with sex or bodies is so far off. But the reality is that raising children who are body and sex positive starts from the beginning.

I grew up in the Bible Belt where a lot of us were raised in the *True Love Waits* culture. I was completely innocent until one random day when I was 12—when I had just had my eyes dilated for the first time. My mom got me a burrito, took me to the edge of a broken bridge, and in my vulnerable state, awkwardly started in on her version of sex-ed. By the time she finished I was in a state of shock. I was scared. I was queasy. I have a feeling she must have felt many of those same feelings as she tried to let me in on subjects that were complex and felt taboo. The whole situation stands out in my mind as such a jarring experience, and honestly not even one that prepared me well for anything at all. My poor mother had gathered the bits and pieces from her mother and the discomfort she felt was palatable. My grandmother on my dad's side once told me that she didn't know anything about what was supposed to happen on her wedding night, so she went to her widowed father to sheepishly ask what to do. All he told her was, "Honey get the rake and scrape the dirt off of the bottom of your feet."

Everyone has their own stories of learning about sex and bodies. Some learned from older siblings or kids at school, some were told really young, and some of my friends were like me and it was whispered about like it was something shameful.

There was a good chance that the generational cycle of shame and hiding regarding sex would have continued through my children except that someone told me early on to just answer my childrens' questions as they asked them— point blank and in an age appropriate way. This avoided a big talk or a feeling of being held out on when they got older. So I did it with all three of my kids. Not perfectly, mind you, but I really did just answer their questions as they came up. No hiding, no shame.

My boys knew what periods were by the time they could

talk and it was so normalized that by middle school, my son took note of his girlfriend's cycle and would walk to the Dollar General a mile from our house to buy her chocolate once a month. I told a woman this, thinking they would feel the same sort of pride I felt, and instead she surprised me and let out a huge groan. "That is disgusting." I was taken aback. It's crazy to me that half of the population menstruates and yet we act like it is some big and dirty secret. My son being clued into the reality of cycles seems like such a step in the right direction and certainly nothing to groan about.

My kids probably got a much higher entrance into normalizing stuff because I was a birth doula and photographer. Sometimes we would have a placenta in our fridge or I would be editing photos of a vaginal birth at the table while they ate a snack as toddlers. I just told them how it was and they have known nothing different.

One time my tiny 5-year-old boy was standing in line at a sandwich shop and was conversing with a woman who looked about 7 months pregnant. "Do you know if you're having a boy or a girl? Are you going to eat your placenta?" he asked—genuinely curious.

On the opposite spectrum, one time I was nursing my baby in the alcove at church and a ten-year-old girl came up to me and gasped, "Ewwwwww what are you doing?!"

"I'm feeding my baby." I said, a little confused as to what all the fuss was about.

Her face stayed twisted as she watched and I said matter of factly, "Yeah that's what boobs are made for."

I couldn't believe a 10-year-old was unaware of this very normal part of life. But also, I could because we tuck nursing moms away from the public, we cover them up, and our children don't see it. This natural thing has become a mystery. We are no longer living in one room homes or in villages where intimacy, bodies, birth, and breastfeeding are normal parts of the being human.

In my experience, things we don't talk about become places where abuse and perversion can more easily take root. Teaching children the correct anatomical name for their body parts alone reduces their risk of sexual grooming and assault.

When we don't, as parents, take the time to talk about big subjects like sex, our children are going to be getting their information elsewhere. I remember perusing the Christian, Focus on the Family web site *Plugged In* as a curious 13 year old who could never dream of bringing up the subject of sex to her parents. It was a website meant to warn Christian parents about the dangers of movies. *Aladdin* was flagged for inappropriate outfits, *Beauty and the Beast* for violence. But I figured out on our dial-up internet, on the thick computer in our shared living room, that if I searched the rated R movies, then I got a pretty descriptive peek into things I wanted to know more about. I snuck around in shame, reading this religious web site like erotica. This grew the feeling of shame connected with sex and arousal for me, which I didn't begin to untangle till late in my 30's.

We are all sexual beings on a spectrum. Our children will be curious. This is a given. But by shying away from talking about the hard things, we are missing such a huge opportunity in creating safety and positivity with our children, giving them a huge leg up in the world.

I told my youngest about sex while we were sleeping on a mattress on the floor, the day we moved into our new home. Lucy was 8 and had recently started expressing concern about getting pregnant. My stories of the births I attended as a doula haunted her. Even though I was exhausted and it felt like an inopportune time to broach the milestone subject of intercourse, I just casually told her that she would not be pregnant because she needed to have intercourse for that.

I remember waiting for the shame, the giggling, the awkwardness. Instead, she just exhaled relief, asked a few clarifying questions, and fell fast asleep.

I think a lot of times we parents put our own shame and complex feelings about sex onto our children, and it doesn't belong there.

We can change the narrative for them. We can raise boys who understand cycles and girls who aren't embarrassed about their bodies. We can equip our children to be healthy sexual adults who know their worth and ask for what they need. It starts with paving a new pathway. It really does start with working through our own hangups and traumas.

20

Include your children in
helping you so that they know
they have a place of
belonging

They were the lumpiest, worst brownies I'd ever tried. But his little face was so bright with pride as he placed the plate of them on our table for dessert. He watched as we managed to swallow bites and hide some in our napkins. 3 hours ago, this child had been an absolute disaster of hitting, kicking, and agitation. I watched him in awe. I hadn't seen this kind of peacefulness in so long. Not only had he provided something for our table, but he had been reminded of his value to our family while doing it.

When I had two young kids, I went to a parenting workshop hosted by a professor who believed that most behavior problems stemmed from children not having a sense of belonging. She had studied untouched, primitive cultures for decades and was always trying to figure out why they didn't seem to have behavior problems with their children. What she noticed and shared with us, was that every child, no matter how young, all had a deep sense of belonging, a sense that their family unit needed them. Children as young as 2 had simple chores to do and they fit perfectly in the working unit of the family. Because of this undeniable sense of belonging, they didn't act out to try to figure out where they belonged. What a stark contrast from the society I'm raising my children in, where parents are glorified servants to their children and our children have frequent tantrums and seasons of acting out—trying to figure out where they fit in. They are constantly pushing the edge of *am I important? Am I needed in this family?* This brief 3-hour workshop had a deep impact on me and I found myself paying attention. When one of my kids was acting out, I stopped what I was doing and would say, "Hey! I need your help with something." 9 times out of 10 the energy would shift and the child would misbehaving immediately. I was shocked! Why didn't more people know about this simple shift?

I started telling my kids, "I couldn't do this without you." and started expecting more out of them with household duties. Their behavior problems quickly reduced when I made an effort to include them in daily life as an integral part. Little chubby hands helped stir dinner, my daughter would fold washcloths into the most uneven little piles, seeds were planted, random snacks that didn't complement each other would be prepared excitedly, and suddenly everyone belonged. Did I have to put aside my desire for perfectly folded washcloths? Yes. Did I have to sweep crumbs from where they had been preparing food? Yes.

I still slip into laziness with this. Usually, it seems faster to do it myself or I don't want to bother them out of their play, but the ripple effects of asking them to contribute to our family by way of setting the table or doing something that is specifically their job are far reaching and positive.

Watch and see how sending a ten-year-old into the store to buy milk (with safety talks and you being nearby of course) changes their attitude. I remember my son, who was in elementary school with severe ADHD and always being the kid in trouble, feeling so good about himself when I sent him in the store for a few things. His wide smile beamed as he loaded his small bag of groceries into the back of the car and I told him how much that helped. All these little deposits of how he helped our family started building up and this child's self confidence started to soar. It wasn't a behavior thing, it was a belonging thing.

My middle child is so different from his brother. He has such a laid-back attitude and is usually not quick to jump in and help. I remember one day in particular needing the grass mowed. I knew Barclay could do it faster and better. I felt tempted to not even ask Sullivan to do it, but I knew that even if I had to push a little, he needed that feeling of belonging and overcoming a challenge too. There was some grumbling and push back, but the reward was how his eyes lit up when he came into the kitchen an hour later—sweaty and covered in grass. I immediately noticed a change in his attitude in the home after that one instance. That confidence trickled into so many other areas.

If I could go back, I would have started as soon as they could walk, I would expect things out of them that maybe seemed too hard, not because I wanted to abuse my power or get things done with free labor, but out of love...out of telling them with my actions and my expectations that our family needed what only they could provide.

21

Wrapping up

I am absolutely positive that in the time this book goes to print, that I will feel like a fraud. Honestly, I've felt like a fraud nearly the whole time I have sat down to even write.

Who do I think I am giving any sort of advice on this job of raising babies?

But I'm convinced that the best parents in the whole world are the ones who feel like frauds; who do their best, while holding space for learning and healing. I do believe that the only thing that parents can agree on is the fact that the learning never stops. Once we "figure something out" our children change. Every single parent is different. Every single child is different. Parenting is one big humbling experience.

My hope in writing this book is not to swoop in and save the day. My hope is that giving you, the parent, permission to not be perfect, to learn, grow, apologize, change your mind...will allow you the freedom to find much joy in the process—because there is much joy to be had.

If you have enjoyed this book would you pretty please take the time to give me a review on Amazon or Goodreads? Not only do I squeal when I read every single one, but it helps boost my book so more people can find it!

Thank you to

Barclay for letting me figure it out and not hating me for the times I didn't get it right. I love spending time with the man you have become.

Sullivan for always letting me hold you even though you're nearly a foot taller than me.

Lucy Miller for telling me you love me 50 times a day and being the best last baby, a mom could ask for.

Jimmy for being the greatest co-parent and partner. Thank you for feeding us, keeping us on track, and planting me pretty wildflowers. I'm so glad to not be alone. In 10 years, we are going to have the best times when they come back to visit. You came just in time.

My mother for giving me so many sweet memories that I will always cherish.

My dad. I always know at least one person in the world loves me no matter what, and it's you.

All my clients past and present for teaching me so many important lessons.

Jimmy's mama for showing me the most beautiful love.

Renee for your check marks that kept me going and for your God given ability to gracefully rearrange my words.

Caroline for knowing my heart.

Kaylee for being the first person to tell me, "PEOPLE NEED THIS BOOK!" You kept me going.

Lily for inspiring the idea to write this book. I love the way you prepared for motherhood.

Flo for the absolutely beautiful ways you elevate my books.

About the Author

Helen Joy is a mess; a beautiful, growing, creative, tender loving mess. She enjoys her children 85% of the time, makes beautiful photos of people who want to remember how things felt, not just what they looked like, does stand up comedy on most Monday evenings, and writes all the freaking time.

Want to connect?

You can read Helen Joy's daily random thoughts on her

Substack:

Notes from An Empty Bathtub @writtenbyhelenjoy.-

substack.com

Or follow her on Instagram @helenjoygeorge

www.helenjoywrites.com